MW00425185

Old Men and Fire: Parables from a Volunteer Firehouse

Gary Kowalski
Hondo Volunteer Fire & Rescue
Santa Fe County, New Mexico

All proceeds from the sale of this book
will benefit Hondo Fire.

Cover photo by David Silver

Copyright © 2017 by Gary Kowalski
All Rights Reserved

ISBN No. 9781521105214

I can think of no more stirring symbol of man's
humanity to man than a fire engine.

Kurt Vonnegut, Jr.

Contents

Old Men and Fire: Neither Aging Nor Firefighting Are For Sissies

When he retired after a long career of teaching English at the University of Chicago, Norman Maclean started to write. *Young Men and Fire*, begun at the age of seventy-four, was published posthumously and won the National Book Critics Circle Award.

The volume you now hold in your hands, *Old Men and Fire,* is a different sort of book, but not entirely.

Though he spent half a century as a professor, Maclean was always a firefighter at heart. At the age of fifteen, he joined the U.S. Forest Service in Montana, chasing blazes and digging firebreaks across the West with a shovel and pick. Fighting wildfires is young men's work. It attracts daredevils, drifters, college boys, and escapees from the nine-to-five or unemployment line who are ready for an adventure at once reckless, rough, romantic and remote.

Firefighting is not for softies.

Reared by a hard-shelled Scottish Presbyterian minister, the author likened the brotherhood of which he was a member to an ecclesiastical order. "Although many Smokejumpers never see each other after they leave the outfit, they remain members of a kind of fraternal organization that also has dim ties with religion." Hearkening back to Calvin's theology, they share a sense of being chosen. Chosen, first, in the sense of being elect or elite: the hombres with the guts and grit to get it done. Chosen, secondly, signifying that these men have some personal business to transact with Fate, God, or the Universe, and the fire line is the locus they have selected for the negotiations to occur.

Maclean wrote *Young Men and Fire* to implement what he called an "anti-shuffleboard" theory of aging. The book revisits the deadly Mann Gulch fire of 1949 which claimed the lives of sixteen Smokejumpers in a sudden blowup, seeking to turn a senseless tragedy into both a scientific study of fire behavior and a tribute to those who perished. For Maclean, it was also an attempt to reckon with his own lost youth, his wife's impending death from cancer, and his personal mortality.

Picking up the pen, for him, was an act of late-life audacity. The professor of literature was "old enough to be scripturally dead," he said, before he dared to become the protagonist of his own story. Students recalled that in his Shakespeare classes, Maclean the academic typically spent the entire first day of class lecturing on the opening lines of

Hamlet, in Act One, Scene One, where the sentry Barnardo cries "Who's there?" It is a question that strikes to our very core.

Who am I? Ego, superego or id? Private person or public persona? Resume or obit? Each of us holds multitudes. I recall a theory that people remain ageless in their subconscious. Our inner self-image doesn't recognize birthdays, or anniversaries, or take account of wrinkles or beer bellies or going bald. Psychically, the I called me has a timeless quality, while in actuality muscles sag, memories fade, and eyesight dims. And growing a soul, forming a sense of self realistic and resilient enough to endure the slings and arrows, is a lifelong endeavour.

The struggle intensifies in times of transition, especially in our later years. How shall we spend the interval remaining? What little can we still do or be or accomplish? Some faiths and cultures provide an honored place for the aged. Old folks in the West, on the other hand, are more likely to feel like nobodies. The problem of self-identity," Maclean wrote, "is not just a problem for the young. It is a problem all the time. Perhaps the problem. It should haunt old age, and when it no longer does, it should tell you that you are dead."

As Maclean says, answering Barnardo's challenge is not just a quandary for young. Close to the age for collecting Social Security, I became a volunteer with the Hondo Volunteer Fire District in Santa Fe, New Mexico. Like many empty-nesters and retirees, I found myself wondering what to do with my time. Clearing brush and household puttering could never be a full time occupation. I had raised a family, had a career, and achieved a modest level of security. The church I'd served as minister in New England for twenty years had called a new pastor and a graceful exit demanded distancing myself from that congregation, which for me meant finding new friends in a new location. I wanted to be useful, but too many volunteer positions in my experience involved busy work or bureaucracy. So I was no longer a parent, a breadwinner, nor a man of the cloth, but what then?

For me, being a fireman was never a childhood dream. I was not chosen for this vocation. But when the fire station near our new home in the foothills of the Sangre de Cristos advertised an open house, my wife and I attended. What I noticed was that a lot of the guys at the station were Baby Boomers like me, past their prime (if not quite yet past their expiration date). Paul Kelly, an EMT and federal judge, is probably our oldest active volunteer at seventy-five, but most are senior citizens. Nationwide, I learned, almost a quarter of active firefighters are past the age of fifty. I thought maybe I could *do* this.

Not only that, as I gained experience, I started to think that maybe I could *be* this. In opinion polls, firefighters rank among the professionals people admire most, jostling consistently for top honors with doctors and military commanders. Prior to volunteering, my own list would have been different. I don't think I'd ever known a fireman or thought about them much. I admired poets and college professors (like Norman Maclean) much more than guys who wore funny hats and pulled kittens out of trees. But as my knowledge of firefighting grew, so did my respect.

The guys I worked with, I discovered, were amazing individuals: artists, race car drivers, journalists, attorneys, guidance counselors and robotics engineers. They were of all political persuasions. Two women complemented our team. What both genders had in common was an all-for-one camaraderie coupled with commitment to upholding certain high standards of conduct along with the hoary traditions of the fire service.

"Having people in my life who would run into a burning building to save me is something few people in life can say," remarked my duty section officer Terry without a trace of irony. Sincerity is mixed with locker room irreverence. "Don't tell me to shut up! It's shut up lieutenant to you!" Terry yelled at me one morning when I told him to get off my back. As a rookie, I found myself wanting to be good enough, smart enough, strong enough to be part of this gang.

I didn't join to wrestle with the Imponderable. I'm different from Norman Maclean in this. I conducted my philosophizing early and have come to fire duty late in life. "Fireman" is an unlikely guise at best and one that brings out my own inner Hamlet, unsure at times how much I only pretend to wear the uniform.

Yet as a clergyman, I tend to see parables and life lessons everywhere. It's a professional hazard for preachers. Whether sitting at a traffic light or speeding down the highway with lights flashing and sirens blaring, the sermonizer is constantly on lookout for the amusing story or instructive incident. So perhaps it was inevitable that I would find deeper meaning amid the deluge nozzles, dump tanks and hydrant wrenches that have become the tools of my new trade.

But to be clear, I didn't volunteer to fight fires in order to write a book about it. I did it to get out of the house.

False Alarms: Being Grateful For Emergencies That Never Happen

Firefighters are trained to save lives. That's why they're called emergency responders. But most of the work they do is inconsequential, boring even. In the most recent calendar year for which statistics are available, for example, fire departments in the U.S. responded to 2,238,000 false alarms.

Two million is not necessarily a bad thing.

People call the fire department for the darndest reasons. One captain told the story of how a junior officer had been dispatched to a home where the occupant worried his stove might catch fire. What seems to be the problem? the fireman asked after entering the kitchen dressed in full protective gear. The man explained that he had an electric range and had spilled a cup of milk on top. Knowing very little about appliances, he was aware that liquids can short an electric circuit. Was the Two Percent an accident waiting to happen?

Modeling courtesy, the fireman listened patiently before responding, Let's see what we can do, and then taking a paper towel he carefully wiped up the milk. The problem seemed to be solved, but the anxious homeowner still wasn't satisfied. What if some of the liquid had leaked down inside? Couldn't the stove catch fire in the night? Not likely, but we can take every precaution, the firefighter offered and proceeded to pull the range away from the wall and unplug it from the outlet. Call an electrician in the morning, he advised with a straight face. The man seemed grateful and happy with the visit. Mission accomplished.

Most emergencies never emerge. I recall one of Garrison Keillor's yarns. The story involved a middle-aged man on a ladder, cleaning the gutters on his two-story house. Somehow the guy mistakes his footing, loses his balance, and tumbles. A first-rate novelist or playwright would take this incident as an opportunity to build drama, the humorist observed. The man bumps his head, for instance, develops amnesia, wanders out of the yard and spends the rest of his lifetime trying to figure out who he is. Or something equally disastrous happens. That's what makes for thrilling narrative. But in this case, the man is hardly hurt at all, aside from a few bruises. He picks himself up, wipes the dirt off his trousers and goes about his routine, barely even noticing how really lucky he has been. Because a hundred times a day, most of us manage to scale ladders without getting a concussion, take showers without slipping in the tub, and cross the street without needing to call 911. And that's the real although under reported story. How lucky we all are not to be living in a first-rate novel but in the tedious world we inhabit where goodness and mercy are commodities too ordinary to be remarked on. How often there's smoke but no fire, or the smoke turns out to be just a little haze on the hillside.

I felt that sense of good fortune the first dozen times my pager rang.   My first run with the Hondo District was for an MVA or Motor Vehicle Accident. A driver skidded off the snowy road, but the car didn't flip and nobody was injured. Most calls routinely turned out to be nothing. A twenty-three year old man asked for the medics because he thought he was having a heart attack when the real problem was he'd just consumed a whole pot of coffee.

Whenever the pager sounds, I race to the station, adrenaline pumping, then usually return home forty-five minutes later having saved no lives and doused no infernos. I try not to resent being called out for no reason, nor regret responding to caffeine crises.

Who needs thrills? Rather I'm grateful for having so little to do, thankful for each banal day the engine doesn't stop in front of my house, glad when the worst that happens is a little spilled milk.

Good Stories: Bad Days Make For Memorable Yarns

"Now it is a strange thing," remarks Tolkien in one of his novels, "but things that are good to have and days that are good to spend are soon told about and not much to listen to; while things that are uncomfortable, palpitating, and even gruesome, may make a good tale, and take a deal of telling anyway." Despite the placid passing of days with no excitement, there's plenty of gore in the line of duty. You are liable to encounter DCAPBTLS, an acronym EMTs use to encapsulate the range of human woe encountered on the fireground: Deformities, Contusions, Abrasions, Burns, Tenderness, Lacerations and Swellings. Not a pretty picture. When I initially expressed interest in volunteering, it was one of the first questions I was asked. Was I up to the task? Could I handle dismemberment and stuff?

I thought I could. Back when I was first contemplating seminary, I'd worked on a suicide hotline in South Boston and recalled a night when I applied pressure to the wounds of a woman who wandered in with two slashed wrists, keeping her from bleeding out until the ambulance arrived. I thought about my clinical pastoral training in a hospital where I'd been summoned to pray over a man charred to a cinder on a crash scene. He didn't survive, but I did. Some men (like my father-in-law, who flew bombing missions over Japan) faint at the sight of blood. Not me. Yet my educated guess is that each of us-- even the most Stoic--has a breaking point.

Consider: one night we were being tutored in the Holmatro device. Holmatro is a company that manufactures a variety of gizmos for getting victims out of a jam, literally: cutters, jacks, spreaders and other gear powered hydraulically (by water pressure or sometimes oil) or pneumatically (by air) to open cars like tin cans. We were learning to use the lifting bags, which are like inflatable pillows, except made of Kevlar. Hooked to the hose on an air tank (the same tank the firefighter carries on his back to breathe inside a burning building), the bag expands with ridiculous force.

When placed under the frame of a disabled vehicle, a small bag (the size of a sofa cushion) can raise 11,000 pounds (roughly two Cadillac Escalades) six or eight inches into the air, just enough wiggle room to extricate a trapped body. The larger bags can hoist over 70,000 pounds, the weight of a semi-trailer truck. I could imagine a motorcyclist sliding under some smoldering wreck on the interstate and getting pinned, helpless. The Holmatro would get him out.

Except be sure to have the paramedics examine him first, we were warned. In one case, the weight of the car on her torso was the only thing holding a woman in one piece. She was conscious and talking. But when rescuers inflated the Holmatro, that was the end. She was cut in half.

What's your breaking point?   Where are your limits? Exactly how much reality can you stand?

Between life and death, between the pleasure of having your hands on the wheel while cruising down life's highway and the "uh-oh" of sensing the tires skidding out of control, there's a very thin line: the frontier of being and non-being. That boundary slices down the center of our existence. Call it the liminal. Like the double yellow line down the middle of the road, it separates time from eternity.

Yet that line can be just as insubstantial as paint on the pavement. I have helped pull bodies burned beyond recognition from the cabs of cars that slammed into oncoming vehicles, when one driver mistakenly headed south on a northbound lane. Melted into the plastic of the dashboard, the torsos had to be removed from their cars with a reciprocating saw. We are so accustomed to hurtling through the world a split second from annihilation that we seldom notice how close we live to the median.

Paul Tillich, the theologian, identified that dotted line as the dimension of finitude or nothingness that bisects every person into a short-lived phenomenon, at once palpably present and already gone. It is the threshold where everything dependable might suddenly slip away. Living on that edge is not necessarily a comfortable place to hang, nor is the fire station.

But it's where the good stories get made.

Keep Breathing: Respiration Equals Inspiration

Ancient people associated breath with life. In Genesis, for example, God shapes Adam's form like a potter shapes a vessel of clay and then, in a primitive version of mouth-to-mouth resuscitation, the deity blows into the man's nostrils, turning him into "a living soul" (in Hebrew, *nefesh chayah*). Nowadays, first responders generally don't do mouth-to-mouth anymore, unless there is a shield available to prevent contagion. Still, it is a great image: the Creator delivering what's come to be known as "the kiss of life." Invisible and always moving, breath to the authors of the Bible (as well as to observers in many other archaic cultures) appeared to be synonymous with vitality and survival.

It's a powerful metaphor but medically misleading, because some kinds of breathing indicate death is near. Agonal breathing falls into this category. It often accompanies cardiac arrest. Agonal breathing is characterized by spasmodic gasps, drawn at irregular intervals by an unconscious patient whose heart has stopped. At an emergency scene, bystanders may describe it as snorting, gurgling, heaving, or moaning as the body strains for air. As the term "agonal" suggests, a struggle is underway. By some measures the victim is already dead.

[20]

Unless normal breathing and a pulse are rapidly restored, the patient soon expires.

My second month on the job, I received a cheat sheet to help decipher the various medical codes that might come over my pager. The number *29* means a traffic accident, for example, while *Delta* means it's bad. The acronyms are an alphabet soup that all spell trouble, from Allergies and Animal Attacks to Assault, Burns, Chest Pain, Convulsions, Drowning, Electrocution, Falls, Hanging, Hemorrhage, and Overdose. "Breathing Problems" are in a class of their own. Agonal breathing, on the other hand, is not categorized as a breathing problem at all, but falls into the same family as Respiratory Arrest.

And/or Death.

Agonal breathing concerns paramedics and firefighters, because telephone dispatchers frequently ask the caller "Is the patient breathing?" to help assess the situation at the other end of the line. A person who is breathing--even if respiration is labored--is generally in good shape. A crying child is a healthy child, in most cases. The lungs are functioning. But agonal breathing indicates an immediate need for medical intervention.

I thought about this at the gym. Twenty minutes on a stair machine can leave me panting. In my sixth decade, catching my breath is a considerable challenge, and I wonder if I'm up for the physical demands of this job. Santa Fe required all its responders to take a physical last spring: I passed, but puffing into the spirometer (which measures lung capacity by blowing into a tube as hard as you can, as fast as you can, and as long as you can) left me light-headed and wheezy.

Then I remember that before the final gasp, each one of us gets a finite number of inhalations on this trip, about 200 million on average, and I climb back on the elliptical. What better way to use my time than learning CPR or simple first aid? *Start compressions. Open airways. Administer breathing.* Respiration conquers death.

Maybe God blew that first magical breath, as the Bible suggests. Perhaps not. Let the theologians and biologists decide how life got started. But for sure, anyone can save a life.

For now, for me, it's a reason to keep on huffing.

Being Nice: Finding A Personal Mission

When I was just starting out in ministry, an older colleague and mentor advised me that ninety-nine percent of my job description was to simply be nice. That counsel was helpful in later years, when I was tempted to lose my patience or my temper, when panhandlers came knocking on the church door, when parishioners angry at God directed their hostility at me, or when a bereaved family just needed someone to witness and understand their grief. Most folks are doing their best under difficult conditions. Even if you can't fix their problem, you can at least listen and pay attention.

Firefighting, I've come to realize, is another form of ministry. As Gregory Widen (who scripted Backdraft) observed, "the funny thing about firemen, night and day, is that they are always firemen." It's not just a living, but a life.

LIke the priest or rabbi, the first responder is on call 24/7 and liable to encounter people at their best and worst. So I wasn't surprised to learn that one big city fire department, in Phoenix, has a mission statement that clergy of all denominations might endorse: *Survive, Prevent Harm, And Be Nice.*

Being nice in Phoenix means going the extra mile and farther. On a medical call, one team arrived to find a middle-aged man keeled over from heavy exertion. He'd been repaving his driveway under the blistering Arizona sun. The EMTs quickly stabilized him and transported the stricken man to the hospital.

But the chief was puzzled when the remainder of the crew failed to return to the station. Time passed and finally the boss went to investigate. Still on the scene, the firefighters had seen the portable mixer filled with wet cement, which left unattended would dry to a rock-hard mass. So they'd decided to finish the repaving the drive. They were assisting in a concrete fashion.

In a similar case, the med unit answered a 911 from a barber shop one day. The stylist had suffered a heart attack in the midst of snipping. As paramedics whisked the hair cutter to the emergency room, the remaining responders finished trimming the patron's locks. Close shave, but with a happy ending.

Here in the Hondo District, I've met some awfully nice guys, like our Assistant Chief, Rich. He and his wife Suzanne were Peace Corps volunteers in Liberia back in the late sixties. When they returned to visit the country fifty years later, they expected to see decades of progress and development. Instead, they witnessed conditions worse than anything they remembered.

Liberia suffered fourteen years of civil war in which nearly a quarter of its people died as the country very literally tumbled into darkness. Only a fourth of its inhabitants were connected to an electric grid. When the sun set, gloom descended. With a per capita income of just $158 per year, most Liberians were paying a quarter of that simply to recharge their cell phones. The country was a wreck

Rich saw both need and opportunity. After a stint at Harvard's Advanced Leadership Initiative that prepares entrepreneurs for post-career service to the world, Rich now heads the Liberian Energy Network, bringing solar power to one of Africa's least developed nations. With electric lights, for the first time, kids can study at night. Fisherman can take advantage of calmer evening seas. Doctors and nurses confronting Ebola have illuminated operating rooms and reliable equipment. Founded in 2011, LEN in its first twelve months lit up 4,300 homes, and with solar panels that cost less than this paperback book, Rich aims to turn Liberia into the first nation on the planet that derives its energy principally from the sun.

That's altruism. For his work, Rich received a "Point of Light" award and has been featured in magazines like *Forbes*. When it comes to charity, the guys at Hondo set a high bar.

What if we all spent more time thinking about our own personal mission statements? LEN's is powerful and to the point: "Seeking not simply to light a house, or to light a village, but to light a nation." Mission and vision statements for corporations and nonprofits have been around for years. But the idea of a personal mission was introduced by author Stephen Covey in his bestselling book on *The Seven Habits of Highly Effective People* where he suggests that in life, as in every worthwhile endeavor, we must keep ultimate ends in mind. "If your ladder is not leaning against the right wall, every step you take gets you to the wrong place faster," as he puts it.

Where is your ladder leaning? What light are you bringing to the dark places? My friend Hersch Wilson, who is medical captain at Hondo, has a simple formula to live by: *Be Brave, Be Kind, Fight Fires.* As he expresses it,

Be Brave. Take risks, live your life, accept what life is: short and astonishing.

Be Kind. For every opportunity firefighters have to be brave, we have one hundred opportunities to be kind.

Fight Fires. We all have and will have problems. The pager will summon us all of our lives. Our task is to solve the problems we face.

Herschel, who has been doing this work for more than twenty years, says that firefighting changed his life, teaching him that "life is short and unpredictable, that there is tragedy and suffering all around," but that despite the brevity and uncertainty of existence, we can choose joy over fear, making kindness and gratitude our first response without expecting payback.

Hersch is twice the firefighter I am and probably three times as wise. I don't even have even have a personal mission statement, truthfully. But I have always remembered and taken to heart that simple advice I received as a young pastor. I try not to be a jerk.

Being Nice has worked for me.

Searching: Hunting For Quarry That Matters

The pager in the bedroom rang at 3:40 am. Because of interference and poor reception, I often have trouble understanding the dispatch. But I caught the phrase I-25 and figured it must be a traffic accident somewhere on the ten mile strip of interstate that runs through our district.

Then we arrived on scene, the City of Santa Fe had already established a presence in the southbound lane that runs into town. From the number of flashing lights, I knew it was something big. As our engine rolled in, I could see a white semi-trailer truck jack-knifed off the road, onto the right shoulder. Then I saw a smaller pickup that had flipped onto its roof, partially crushed, sitting upstream of traffic in the middle of the highway. Apparently the pickup rolled first and the eighteen-wheeler braked and swerved to avoid a collision.

The driver on the big rig had already been transported to the hospital with glass in his eyes. But whoever was driving the pickup, or whatever passengers might have been inside, were missing. Blood in the cab was all that remained to say there had been serious injuries.

Seatbelt safety gets drilled hard at fire school. The days when firefighters careened around corners standing on the running boards of their engines, hanging on for dear life, are gone, but every year several die when they are ejected from their vehicles in high speed collisions. They weren't buckled up.

So with flashlights we began to search of the adjoining right-of-way on the theory that the driver had been thrown from the cab, potentially landing far from the crash site. The National Highway Traffic Safety Administration limits the energy load that occupants can experience in a car traveling thirty miles an hour smashing into a rigid barrier to thirty G's of force. For a typical driver weighing 150 pounds, that's equivalent to getting whacked with thirty times their body mass, or like being hit with a pile driver packing 2 ½ tons of punch. When the vehicle is traveling at sixty miles an hour, that figure quadruples. With that kind of impact, our guy could be anywhere.

Our search spread far from the tarmac into the dried thickets of chamisa and juniper that flanked the roadway. Six of us from Hondo combed the area. We had a thermal imaging cameras to help, that seek out heat. Yet the only signs of life (or death) were a bleached rib cage from a roadkill deer and a few enormous anthills. I was warm in my bunker gear, but glad the night time temperatures are brisk in the high desert this time of year. No snakes.

Two hours later, back home in bed, I was shivering. Without my realizing, the cold had crept in. I thought of all the hours I'd spent searching over the course of my lifetime, often in futility: as a young man searching for faith and answers, then as a senior citizen coping with "old-timers" disease, searching for car keys, check books, eyeglasses, names I can't remember and faces I can't quite place.

What is it we spend our whole lives seeking? Maybe the hunt is the point, especially in the small hours. To be awake and alert, on the lookout. Not to slumber or sleep-walk our entire existence but extend our senses into our surroundings, scouting the territory, penetrating what's hidden. To stalk quarry that actually matters, not for sport, but in life-or-death earnest. To be of use.

We never did locate the driver of the pick-up. According to dispatch, he somehow walked away from the wreck and wandered into the hospital while we were still scouring the pitch dark scrub. We packed up and packed it in. But despite that, I think I found something valuable last night, better than car keys and probably more satisfying than any creed: an experience of being alive.

Save the Shoes: Small Actions Make A Difference

I was first on scene, where the proprietor of a local eatery had just phoned 911. A young man named Jesse had wandered into the diner, shoeless and incoherent, He'd taken something--ecstasy or meth--but wasn't sure what. Meanwhile, the flesh from his big toe was badly cut away and probably needed stitches. Eventually the medics came and carted Jesse to the hospital, but not before I found his dented red pickup in the parking lot, retrieved his tattered work boots from the floorboard and stuck them in the ambulance for the ride. He needed footgear.

It made me think of another firefighter, Mark Bezos, who has a paid job with Robin Hood Foundation, an anti-poverty organization located in New York City. When he's not attacking homelessness or hunger, he's usually battling blazes as the Assistant Captain for Volunteer Fire Company No. 2 in nearby Scarsdale.

He also gives a mean speech. In 2011, Mark delivered a TED Talk that has been seen over a million times by online viewers around the world.

On stage, dressed in his heavy bunker gear, Mark looks a lot like the guys from Hondo: fifties, balding, stubbled chin, masculine but on the mature side. He describes how rapidly he has to report to a fire if he wants to see any action. There are about eighty volunteers in Scarsdale, supporting the thirty career firemen. Usually, the paid professionals are first on the scene and are in charge of the situation.

That was the case with his very first fire. Mark was the second volunteer to show up, after the pros had established their Incident Command. Still, wanting to put his new skills to use he sought out the Captain directing the operation.

When Mark found him, the Captain was deep in conversation with the homeowner, who was having what could mildly be described as a no good, terrible, very bad night. She was outdoors in her nightgown, beneath an umbrella, in the rain, barefoot, watching smoke billow from her house and flames consume all her earthly possessions.

The other volunteer was there, too, already with the Captain. By a matter of seconds, he'd beaten Mark to the punch. With a mixture of dismay and envy, Mark listened as the Captain gave orders to his brother firefighter: Your job is to go into the house and rescue the dog.

The dog! Golden Retriever? Collie? Dandie Dinmont Terrier? No matter. There went Mark's big chance to shine ... to do valiant deeds ... to tell stories to his grandchildren about how he's saved a living, breathing creature from the flames. Instead, all the credit would go to some other chap -- probably an investment advisor or hedge fund manager entirely unworthy of the the honor. (This was Westchester County, after all.) Bezos had come a moment too late for glory.

Instead, the Chief told Mark that he should go upstairs and get the woman something to put on her feet. Matching action to word, the disappointed firefighter marched into the house and upstairs, past the "real" firemen who had the blaze knocked down by this time, down the hall and into the master bedroom where he found a pair of slippers, which he brought back outside and delivered as asked. Footwear safe and secure! The homeowner, naturally overjoyed to be reunited with her dog, hardly seemed to notice.

Then a few weeks later, the Chief of the Department received a hand-written thank you from the woman whose house had burned. She was most profuse on one point. Amid the incredible stress of doing their jobs -- coping with heat, exhaustion, danger and darkness -- one volunteer had gone above and beyond all duty, being so thoughtful as to bring her sandals.

Save the shoes! As I stuck Jesse's old boots into the ambulance, I realized I'd never be getting a card, hand-written or otherwise. I hadn't done anything courageous or extraordinary. In my brief transition from pastor to first responder, I'd gone from saving souls to salving soles. But maybe someday Jesse's feet--his dogs--would thank me.

Small actions make a difference, and you never know how your actions are affecting others. That's the lesson Mark Bezos drew from his experience. Don't defer kindness. Because the time to help is now. The place to help is here. The person who needs you is the one closest at hand, barefoot or shod.

Ready or Not: Knowing Your Own Limits

Walking into a burning building takes nerve, and when it was his turn, my friend Ed froze on the nozzle. My classmates and I at the Volunteer Fire Academy--where we rookies spent fourteen weeks learning how to be firefighters--were drilling on our first live burn inside a steel structure that consisted of two metal shipping containers welded together to form a T. Literally, we were playing with fire. The crude compartment looked more like a live-in dumpster than a home ablaze, but filled with pine pallets and wet straw, it could generate plenty of heat and smoke. The skies overhead were cloudy and spitting rain, yet the foul weather did little to cool the steel walls that were glowing orange even at mid-day. Our assignment as cadets was to enter this furnace by make-shift doors hacked into the walls, find the fire and put it out.

One of the lieutenants at Hondo told me that somebody in our class would flip or freak out, have a panic attack, or discover they were claustrophobic at the first burn. That person turned out to be Ed, who was supposed to lead the way in with the fog nozzle, hit the hot gases in the upper layer, wait for the steam and cooled smoke to descend and then direct a spray out a window which would act as an exhaust, ventilating the interior and allowing his

[36]

squad to locate the actual seat of combustion. Ed just couldn't do it. His nerves wouldn't tell his muscles what to do. The sight of all that dark chaos immobilized him

Some inner voice told him he had business there.

This was not a matter of courage. It took guts to be the one guy in a class of twenty testosterone-filled, wannabe hose jockeys to bow out -- guts plus a certain level of self-knowledge and maturity. Most of the guys in the Academy are barely beyond their teens, but Ed is the one cadet who's my senior. A retired professor of art from Williams College, he and his wife moved to a tiny village about twenty miles south of Santa Fe to paint. Like me, Ed is a little overeducated, slightly thicker than he needs to be around the middle, not as spry as the twenty-year-olds in the class, but eager to get involved in town affairs and serve his new community.

Yet there are plenty of ways to serve without racing into a blazing building. Ed can still pull people from wrecks, fight brush fires, do search-and-rescue. At graduation, he will be fully certified wear a black helmet, the insignia of a volunteer qualified to "go interior." He simply chooses not to.

When my turn comes, I don't know how I'll fare. Our squad didn't venture in today. I was assigned to the

Rapid Intervention Team. Standard procedures demand two firefighters do RIT, prepped and waiting at a safe distance, ready to intervene if anything goes bad inside.

But shortly our whole class heads to Socorro, home of the state fire training center, where we practice with real flames in a reinforced concrete shell loaded with combustibles like wood pallets doused in kerosene. You crawl around inside on your hands and knees, because it's cooler near the floor. Smoke and darkness limit vision. It's easy to get lost.

It gets wet, too. Water expands in volume 1700 times when it evaporates, so the hose stream hitting the hot gases generates a good facsimile of riding "Maid of the Mist" at the bottom of Niagara, except the moisture is at the boiling point. Too little water and you won't put out the fire. Too much and you suffer steam burns. Temperatures inside, according to our instructor, can soar to fourteen hundred degrees. The face shield on our air masks melts at seven hundred. What could possibly go wrong?

Frankly, I'm scared. But what you fear, said the poet William Stafford, will not go away. Instead, it "will take you into yourself and bless you and keep you." (Stafford should know. He worked as a firefighter during the last world war.)

I suppose this is one reason why people base jump, or free climb, or pit themselves against rock and gravity or fire. It is why they swim with sharks or run marathons or get themselves shot into space. They want to know how they will hold up under pressure, test their limits. They are obeying the Socratic dictum, "Know Thyself."

A few days ago, I was crazy with anxiety, feeling totally insecure, jelly jointed, overwrought, but at some point a switch flipped inside my brain. Now I'm ready to burn. Anticipating turning theory into practice. Confident and eager, prepared for my trial by fire. I'm jazzed, pumped, psyched. At least I think I am.

And what is it that I'll discover about myself when I face my insecurities and the moment of truth arrives? I won't know until I get there.

Interstate: Enjoying The Ride

There is a legendary character named Interstate Ike. Not his real name, but he is a real person, although somewhat mythical, too. Ike is renowned for walking the highway between Albuquerque and Santa Fe (roughly sixty miles), turning around, and then hiking back again. Passing motorists will occasionally phone emergency services when they spot him sleeping near the shoulder, falsely imagining that he might be dead or injured. Hondo has been notified several times when Ike decided to take a nap on our short stretch of I-25. But by the time our guys can get a truck to the area where he was last seen, Ike has invariably woken up and moved on. He is a little like yeti or the Loch Ness Monster in that way, often glimpsed but hard to pin down. Thus his phantasmal reputation.

Presumably Ike has some psychiatric issues, like so many of the homeless who wander our streets. Yet Ike's saunterings are not aimless, just repetitive, as are many journeys through life.

How many of us commute each morning from the suburbs into the city, come back home at night, then wake up to do it again the next day? Watch the six o' clock news, shake our heads in perplexity, then tune into the very same broadcast twenty-four hours later? Work, eat, sleep, repeat. These are the operating instructions for many a career, many a marriage, many a lifetime.

And we suppose Ike is crazy? At least he sets his own schedule. He doesn't have to program his alarm for 5:00 am to make time to visit the gym before showing up at the office, because he gets plenty of exercise, fresh air and sunshine without a *fitbit* or personal trainer. What kind of society imagines that walking on an indoor treadmill for half an hour is a sign of good health, while rambling down a valley corridor, flanked by the Jemez mountains with vistas of the Sandias, is a symptom of mental disorder? Probably the kind of society that encourages folks to stick to the treadmill forever.

Ike inspires me now that I'm retired, because most of my life I've done what's expected. I've been goal driven and task oriented, pushing myself to get ahead. While a few of my dreams have been achieved, most gone by the wayside. But it's too late now to chart a brand new course. What's been has been. The destination no longer means as much. I'm in no rush to reach the the finish line. Most of my milestones are behind me. I have more yesterdays than tomorrows. It's enjoying the remainder of the trip that is foremost.

Probably I'm romanticizing a chap who has some serious ailments. We all have our demons, Ike included. But I like to picture him watching the people whizzing by in their gas-propelled buggies, all in a hurry to get somewhere, asking himself whether he should pull one of those roadside assistance boxes, summoning the responders with the flashing red lights to cope with this mania for going places. If I try hard, I can even see him carrying a copy of *Leaves of Grass* in his hip pocket, afoot and carefree, effusions of light clothing him from head to toe, singing and celebrating the open road.

It Takes A Family: What Money Cannot Buy

Hondo doesn't really do search and rescue. The county has a special unit trained to find missing hikers or aircraft that have vanished into the outback. But sometimes we get called anyway, and when the dispatch comes, it is often to a house on Comanche Ridge.

We have been to that address on multiple occasions. It always seems to be pitch dark and frequently cold. Our first visit was to track down a missing nine-year-old boy. Though the temperature was below freezing, with a dusting of snow, he had been gone for a couple of hours before anyone thought to notify the authorities.

The truck we call Rescue 1 is equipped with a light tower, pumping out several thousand watts from its cantilevered array of halogen lamps, so we set it blazing in the road fronting the house as a beacon, should the child be lost and trying to find his way back. Then with our own hand held streamlights, half a dozen firefighters began combing the surrounding acres of juniper and scrub.

It was hopeless, of course. Juanito, we learned from his grandmother, had a history of running away. His mom, who lost custody after some history of drug abuse, lived miles to the north. The boy had once managed to hitchhike there by himself. What kind of driver picks up a nine-year-old thumbing on the highway? You don't want to know.

But it was obvious we were not going to find a child who didn't want to be found, who might be hiding in any shadow. Still, it was our job to keep looking as the night wore on. Finally, he revealed himself. Juanito had been asleep all the while, cuddled under a stack of blankets in the rear seat of a neighbor's car.

Then a few months later, Juan bolted again, only this time he took his three-year-old sister with him. Footprints showed they were headed in the direction of the highway. Now the sheriff's office and state police were alerted. Search-and-Rescue brought dogs. I rode shotgun in a tanker, cruising the road headed toward town with a directional spotlight illuminating the shoulder, scanning for signs of wayward kids.

When the dogs finally tracked the pair, the boy and his sister were almost three miles from home, hiding in the parking lot behind a local diner. They had eluded their would-be rescuers for hours. Standing on the asphalt, surrounded by squad cars, ambulances, and fire engines, the children appeared small and fragile (as indeed they were), unlikely centers of attention to be surrounded by so many flashing lights. How could a little girl with a pink pony backpack rouse such rumbling machinery into motion?

The kids were far from being delinquents. They were much too tiny. Yet no crystal ball was needed to see how both might end up as juvenile offenders -- once again hunted by police, but for very different reasons.

It occurred to me that these youngsters had a whole bureaucracy at their beck-and-call. The cost to the county and the taxpayers for that one night excursion must have run to thousands of dollars. And behind the immediate ranks of first responders stood a complex phalanx of guardians, social workers and courts to keep these youngsters safe and out of trouble. But there are some things money can't buy and that even the most skilled professionals can never provide. I sensed that whatever happened to Juanito and his sister would probably depend more on their *abuela* and *la familia* than on any number of cops, guidance counselors, or underpaid volunteers like me.

It takes more than a village, I realized, feeling helpless. To raise a child, you need a family too.

Firewalking: Fears Real And Imaginary

Which of our fears and insecurities are reality-based? How many of our worries are purely imaginary? It is not always easy to tell. The scariest scenario imaginable on a wildland blaze is a flame vortex or fire tornado, for example. In contrast, the things that make me jittery are ridiculous, like finding a pair of 100% cotton socks (no polyester blends) that won't melt on the fireground. You wouldn't believe how many brands include spandex. Probably nobody ever died from improper hosiery.

Still, to be on the safe side, I just paid $320 for a pair of National Fire Protection Association approved boots. The shoes are one hundred percent leather, with no man-made materials except for the Vibram, lugged sole. Even the laces are rawhide. You don't want synthetics that will melt in a forest fire, or glue that might delaminate at high temperature, allowing the soles to separate from the upper. These hush puppies can take the heat.

Years ago, I had a clergy friend named Bill who told me about his experience with firewalking. He attended a spiritual retreat where participants tiptoed barefoot across a bed of glowing coals. Bill said that when his turn arrived to tread the fiery walkway, he had a sudden perceptual

[46]

shift. The embers appeared to be an alleyway of luminous cobblestones, kind of like Dorothy's yellow brick road. (What was he taking, I wonder?) Before he was ordained, Bill earned his Ph.D. in chemistry, but he definitely had a mystical streak. For him, the firewalk proved some point about quantum mechanics, how our minds can create various versions of reality where burning coals aren't so hot any more.

Yet apparently, you can stride on embers unscathed even without believing in mind-over-matter. We've been learning in Fire Academy, for example, that there are three ways for heat to propagate, through conduction, convection and radiation. As it happens, wood is a poor conductor. Skillets used to have wooden handles for this reason, before silicone and other heat-resistant plastics were invented. When your bare soles touch the charcoal in a firewalk, not much thermal energy is transmitted, therefore, particularly when the wood is covered with a film of ash. Strolling across a ten or twelve foot bed of coals, your tootsies may be in direct touch with the cinders for less than a second. That's not enough time for serious burns to occur. Ordinary physics (not quantum physics) can explain the seemingly inexplicable.

So it turns about that firewalking is more about overcoming personal fears than anything spooky or metaphysical. And goodness knows, I could use more self-

[47]

confidence. I'm a bundle of anxieties. Still, I'm not eager to have my booties fall apart when the ground starts to smoke. On a wildland blaze, the fire goes subterranean. Roots, old stumps, deep duff and buried logs all begin to smolder. Sometimes you step into a pit where the substrate beneath the forest floor has simply turned to ashes. Hotshots fire walk all the time. They just don't go shoeless.

Though the price is about four times what I've ever paid for footwear, and these Redwings are not the most comfortable things on the planet, I accept the cost. Because there are plenty of real worries on the fireground without manufacturing any extras. There is much more to fear than fear itself. And whether or not I have the right stuff mentally to be a fireman, I will definitely need stuff that is right. I'm much more courageous in a pair of good boots.

Dharma: Life Is Suffering, So Get Over It

With enough heat and a little oxygen, everything burns. Soot, smoke, particulates, carbon monoxide and even the products of burning burn

In his "Fire Sermon," the Buddha addressed a thousand monks with a caution that could have come straight from a firefighter's Bible.

Bhikkhus, all is burning. Burning with what? Burning with the fire of lust, with the fire of hate, with the fire of delusion. I say it is burning with birth, aging and death, with sorrows, with lamentations, with pains, with griefs, with despairs.

Existence is a conflagration of loss and woe. So says the *Pali Canon*. The literal meaning of Nirvana is to be blown out or extinguished, like a candle that has consumed itself and left no remnants. Everything incinerates.

Even heroism burns.

In 1987, firefighter and paramedic Robert O'Donnell became an instant celebrity when he rescued eighteen-month old Jessica McClure from a well where she had become entrapped more than twenty feet below the ground near her home in Midland, Texas. For three days, the nation forgot to care about the crashing stock market or tensions in the Middle East as news crews breathlessly followed the toddler's race against time while extrication teams rammed a parallel shaft through sheer bedrock to reach the child who became known as Baby Jessica. The pipe encasing her was just eight inches in diameter. Occasionally rescuers could hear the toddler crying. At one point, she was heard singing to comfort herself: Winnie-the-Pooh, Winnie-the-Pooh. But no one could see Jessica. As she slowly dehydrated and lost body mass, the youngster was in danger of slipping even farther out of reach.

Tall and lanky, 29 years old with a seven-year-old boy and three-year-old girl of his own, fireman O'Donnell volunteered to squirm through the black, narrow passageway that was finally completed fifty-eight hours after the toddler's disappearance. He was off-duty when the mishap came over the radio, but thought he could help. Drillers had excavated a rescue shaft twenty-nine feet straight down, then bored a thin horizontal tunnel to a point just below the depth they believed Jessica to be wedged.

Lying on his back with a miner's headlamp, the six foot, 145 pound O'Donnell writhed into the rocky crevasse. With painful effort, he could extend a single arm upward into the well to grope for the missing child. He was underground more than an hour. Armed with a tube of lubricating K-Y Jelly, he was finally able to grab Jessica by the heel and inch the terrified youngster to back safety.

He was a media sensation with parades in his honor. He received a letter from the President and a handshake from the VP, as well as countless invitations for interviews.

Whip Hubley, a Hollywood actor cast to play O'Donnell in a made-for-TV movie titled *Everybody's Baby*, quizzed the daring firefighter about his role. "He told me it was just agonizing down there . . . claustrophobia, the physical pressure on your chest. You really felt like you were in a grave."

The gallant rescuer himself had a minor speaking role in the production, playing a news reporter. Gathered with his buddies to watch his film debut, O'Donnell was filled with anticipation and excitement, announcing repeatedly that his part was coming up shortly. However, his part never came. Without his knowledge, his appearance had been edited out of the film, left on the cutting room floor.

By that time, his moment of fame had passed too. No more appearances on Oprah. No more invitations to the White House. Robert O'Donnell was not a celebrity but a medic and ordinary fireman once more, on his way to a divorce, a reprimand from the department for substance abuse, and a career in ashes.

Eight years after the dramatic rescue, he blew his head off with a shotgun.

"I almost put Robert in the category of some of the guys who came back from Vietnam," said his brother, Ricky. "To tell you the truth, I think if he could have, if he had it to do all over again, he would have stayed home and let somebody else help that kid."

That kid, Jessica McClure, is now a happily married, stay-at-home mom, still living in Midland, less than two miles from where she fell down the well. When she turned 25, in 2011, she received access to a trust fund of over $800,000 that poured in from a concerned public during her brief ordeal.

The trust fund for Robert O'Donnell's children amounted to just $815.

As Vietnam vet Tim O'Brien observes, "Everything is combustible. Faith burns. Trust burns. Everything burns to nothing and even nothing burns. The state of Kansas, the forests, the Great Lakes, the certificates of birth and death, every written word, every sonnet, every love letter. Memory burns, and with it all the past and all that ever was. The reasons for burning burn. Flags burns. Liberty and sovereignty and the Bill of Rights and the American Way. It just burns. And when there is nothing, there is nothing worth dying for, and when there is nothing worth dying for, there is nothing."

"Life sucks" was how Robert O'Donnell put it in a hand-scrawled suicide note found in his pickup truck. Life is suffering, the First Noble Truth. Everything ends in dissolution. That's Dharma. But even as I write these words, the pager in my pocket vibrates and I rise from my chair to respond. Toddler trapped in a well? Probably not, yet often I won't know for certain until I get there. It could be anyone …

A hunter with a broken leg, on a remote forest road.

A furnace overheating, just about to set an empty classroom ablaze.

A senior citizen on a nebulizer whose electricity has gone out.

Usually the calls are routine, occasionally scripted for the silver screen (like a man stabbed with scissors in his chest, blood spattered on floors, walls, everywhere!) Yet whenever the pager sounds, I answer if possible, because that's what firefighters do.

Like a bhikku or monk, we follow a path and adhere to a discipline. The bhikku is compassionate. The bhikku vows to rescue other beings from suffering, without exception … like the firefighter.

And that is Dharma, also.

Those Who Have Ears: Coping With Our Own Disabilities

I was impressed when Ben took his ear off in class. Our instructor at Fire School, Captain Lovell, announced to the assembly that Benjamin had some personal information he wanted to impart. The gist of it was that his right ear, which appeared to be misshapen like the rest his jaw line on that side, covered in skin that was rough, reddened and seemly scarred, was only a prosthesis. It was made of plastic, skillfully crafted to look like a real appendage but glued on and removable. I hadn't realized.

We were approaching the final weeks of the Academy, when we were ready to begin practice with our air masks and harnesses. Ben wanted us to know that he would be removing his ear during these skills sessions to insure a smooth seal between the mask's gasket and the rest of his face. He demonstrated peeling the artificial flesh down away from his hairline the way you or I might strip off a large, bulky bandage. Ben didn't want anybody on his squad to be startled or surprised by this unusual maneuver. He had been born with some defects in his palate that were only partially correctable through surgery. Missing an ear was a disability that had no impact on his capacity to function on a fire scene. His fellow cadets, he knew, just needed to get used to the situation and accept it, as he himself had learned to live with it long ago.

Ben spoke matter-of-factly and calmly, in a manner designed to reassure the rest of us. He spoke with the slurred and slightly garbled enunciation that marked most of his conversation. It was the first thing you noticed about Ben, who started volunteering with Hondo just a few weeks after me.

I hate to admit this, but initially I thought he might be a little slow. Ben drove a beat-up pickup equipped with a snowplow, the rear cargo compartment usually jumbled with the tools of his trade as a handy-man. He wore scruffy clothes, not the white collar type. And yes, even people like me who should know better fall into the mistaken notion that problems with speech equate to deficits in thinking. Ben soon disabused me of such misconceptions.

I am not sure if Ben and I were tops in our class, but close to it when it came to written exams. Yet Ben just seemed to intuit the practical aspects of our work that so often elude me. Later, I learned that Ben is an Eagle Scout. He had already done courses in wilderness first aid before starting with Hondo . He runs seventeen mile cross-country races on mountain trails. In other words, Ben is a natural.

Although it takes most volunteers, including me, about a year to move through the probationary steps of becoming a full member of the Hondo Fire Department, Ben did it in half that. Now, while I am still trying to get the basics under my belt, Ben is in school again, this time to become licensed as an Emergency Medical Technician. Still, his attitude is as singular as his aptitude. While many others at Hondo have greater seniority, it is Ben I turn to when I need help, which is often. Because, unexpectedly, I have a learning disability, or what feels like one.

I'm not quick at this firefighting game. Actually, I'm a slow learner. Operating the air compressor? Restoring suction when the pump loses prime? Backing the behemoth trucks into the narrow bays? They didn't teach these things in divinity school, where I studied Old Testament and the Church Fathers. I only wish my dysfunctions were hidden or "invisible," but my blunders are all too evident nearly every time I show up for duty. Gradually, I am getting the hang of this business, yet I know many in the department consider me the special needs kid, the dummy. Sometimes I get yelled at. At times I feel like quitting, dropping out.

Ben is the one of the few guys who can offer instruction and support without making me me feel like a doofus.

Who do you suppose has the bigger disability? Ben, or people like me who judge others by superficial appearances? Since meeting Ben, I've become aware of others like Bryan Stoker, who lost his arm in a car accident, but works as a paramedic with an ambulance company in California while also volunteering as a firefighter like his dad. Or Tommy Barber, of Fort Pierce, Florida, whose glaucoma cost him his vision, but whose training and instincts as a former fireman kicked in when he smelled smoke coming from a neighbor's apartment. Being blind didn't stop him from dousing the flames with an extinguisher or pulling his friend—who had fallen asleep with a pot on the stove—from out of harm's way. We are only as handicapped as our prejudices.

Those who have ears, let them hear.

Friendly Fire: Life From The Ashes

In the early days of the U.S. Forest Service, fire was considered the enemy, plain and simple. A century later, attitudes have changed, along with our understanding of wildland ecology. Fires remove underbrush, open the understory to sunlight, enrich soils, reduce pests, and are actually necessary for the germination of many species like the manzanita. Forest fires are now viewed as potential allies, not always antagonists, in promoting more fertile, abundant forms of life.

Still, it was startling to hear my clergy buddy Greg describe the conflagration that destroyed his Monterey apartment in those terms. He had been living in the two-story complex not far from the ocean, together with his wife and their pets, when the fire ignited. He's still not sure of the cause, only that it was the most traumatic and transforming experience of his life--one that has given him a bond with everyone who has ever survived such a holocaust and that continues to shake and shape him five years after it occurred.

Greg had turned off his phone and was attending a meeting at church when a runner delivered the breathless news that his home was aflame. Most worrisome, the messenger indicated that no one could locate his cat Blanche, whom he had taken in sixteen years before when she was a feral kitten, footsore and hungry.

Greg rushed homeward, where he discovered that emergency personnel had already blocked off the street where four big engines were parked outside apartment complex. Neighbors and bystanders crowded the fireline for a closer look at the sooty plumes rising from the building.

Then he spotted his wife, Liz, sobbing, walking toward him and cradling a small bundle in her arms. The explanation was heartbreakingly simple. Blanche hid under a sofa when the flames broke out. Seeking safety and refuge, the cat had suffocated in the smoke.

"What is that precious thing you imagine carrying when you stand in the midst of your own Armageddon?" Greg asks. "When the security of all that is sacred to you has been breached?"

I took the blanket with Blanche in my arms and held it against my chest. We sat down together on the steps – surrounded by the fire trucks and radios and chaos and the end of the world as we knew it – and wept.

But the universe, so utterly dark at that point, began to show hints of light.

What touched Greg most immediately were the firefighters. As they exited the gutted remains, carrying their hose and pry bars back to the trucks, each one took time to pause and share a word of personal sympathy with the traumatized couple. No, Greg explained to me, Blanche had not been named for the character in the Tennessee Williams drama who depends on the kindness of strangers. But these unexpected expressions of solace from the lips of unknown responders brought incalculable comfort.

Then material aid began to flow. Cash, clothing, toiletries, meals, and the offer of places to stay, along with hundreds of messages of support started to appear, spontaneously and without asking.

"That's what it means to be swept up. That's what it means to be saved," Greg later reflected. Although he had been a minister, like me, for many years, he found himself spiritually rejuvenated in the weeks and months that followed. Though he wasn't entirely sure how the blaze began, Greg stopped smoking. With an insurance settlement adequate to replace most of what had been destroyed, he nonetheless began to re-evaluate his previous attachment to many of his earthly possessions. The items he valued most (like Blanche and several sketch books from his youth) were irreplaceable. Nothing would compensate for their destruction - except for his deepened understanding that the most important things in life can never merely be things.

Greg described the change in the same vocabulary foresters employ to delineate the life giving of effects of forest fire: a cleansing, a scarifying, a necessary purgation. The fire nearly killed him. Nothing could be have been more frightful or disturbing. Burning and especially the thought of being burned trigger an elemental horror. Yet the fire cleared the undergrowth that was stifling his own becoming.

The manzanita, which covers the chaparral from California to New Mexico, looks like an evergreen shrub. The thick, leathery leaves range in hue from a glossy emerald to sage. Yet nothing is perpetually verdant. The hard seeds lie dormant for years, until there is enough blistering heat to split the stubborn husk. Sometimes, Greg learned, we too must be scorched and laid bare to germinate anew.

Departmental: For People Who Care Too Much

Firefighting has been a series of firsts for me. First time behind the wheel in a big red truck. First time on the nozzle. First corpse.

I'm still tired, though it happened yesterday. Administering CPR takes a lot of exertion. You burn one hundred sixty-five calories in fifteen minutes, according to the people who calculate that kind of thing. But the urgency adds stress, which feels exhausting. One tech is injecting epinephrine, another holding a bag with saline drip. A third firefighter is printing cardiac rhythms off a portable Life-Pak, the medic watches waveforms, a fifth volunteer pumps air from a breathing bag, as still another on a stopwatch times one-hundred-twenty second intervals. Meanwhile I'm pushing down fast and hard, open-palmed, on the patient's sternum. Others step in to relieve me, then it's my turn again, like athletes in a relay. This goes on for forty-five minutes.

This is not like practicing on a dummy in the classroom. The woman has no heartbeat, no pulse. Her airway has been suctioned and the room smells like vomit. I'm crouched over her on the floor, directly over her chest, so that I have a choice: either to look into her eyes, which are caramel colored but glazed and unblinking, or to look at her boobs, which have been half-exposed since we hitched up her jersey to get the electrodes into place. So I look nowhere, or focus my gaze on the red electronic numerals from the Life-Pak that help me gauge the proper rate for delivering compressions. I remember constantly that this is a person, about the same age as my sister, if I had a sister. A unique individual with a loving husband who is standing helplessly nearby. Perhaps a mother with children ... but that's too much information.

For while she is a person, I don't want to personalize her. Because she may be a person no longer. From the way Fritz, our paramedic, is talking, we won't be transporting her. He is factual. Initially, there was an agonal ventricular rhythm: the last sign of organized electrical activity in the heart. But that remnant has now vanished. Fritz becomes solicitous. Is there anyone the husband would like him to call? Friends, family members, clergy? The husband is dazed. What now? Fritz is reassuring. Law enforcement is on the way. A medical investigator will remove the body.

Like in the movies, a medic closes the woman's eyelids with his fingertips. She is covered with a blanket. The husband kneels beside his wife, holds her hand, removes her wedding ring.

If I were a pastor, I now would offer a hug and shoulder to cry on. I would ask for a prayer. But that is not my job here. I am an emergency responder, realizing that I would be a pretty lousy firefighter if I didn't care about this woman, but that I would be an even worse one if I allowed myself to care too much. It's a fine line.

Robert Frost has a poem about death in an ant colony, which stands for this regimented, compartmentalized society of ours.

> Ants are a curious race;
> One crossing with hurried tread
> The body of one of their dead
> Isn't given a moment's arrest --
> Seems not even impressed.

But that ant, trading pheromones, reports the incident to another higher up and so on, setting the bureaucracy in motion.

> And presently on the scene
> Appears a solemn mortician;
> And taking formal position
> With feelers calmly atwiddle
> Seizes the dead by the middle,
> And heaving him high in the air

Carries him out of there.

As with the ants, so with the page yesterday. Everyone was professional, helpful, efficient, but somewhat cool, rather emotionally disengaged. "It couldn't be called ungentle," the poet ruefully concludes. "But how thoroughly departmental." Dispatch code Echo (Immediately Life Threatening) is now a code Omega (Beyond Care), and I am figuring out how to be sad about that, understanding it's all in a day's work.

Everyday Heroes: Why Some People Risk Their Lives For Others

If not quite a household name, Lenny Skutnik is a genuine American hero. Born in a small town in rural Mississippi, he held down a variety of jobs while growing up: burger flipper, house painter, supermarket clerk. Skutnik punched a clock in a meat packing plant and worked in a furniture factory, unsung and uncelebrated. But he was employed as an assistant in the printing division of the Congressional Budget Office in 1982 when he stepped out of his quotidian existence and did something extraordinary, the January day that an Air Florida passenger jet attempting to land at National Airport in Washington, D.C slammed into a bridge over the Potomac River and plunged into the icy water.

Most of the eighty-three passengers were killed on impact, but there were a few survivors, struggling to exit the wreckage as they navigated a turbid channel clotted with dead bodies, mechanical debris, spilt luggage, and churning with jet fuel.

Immediately, bystanders who happened on the scene sprang into action. Roger Olian, a sheet metal foreman at a local hospital, fashioned a makeshift rope woven from battery cables, women's scarves and pantyhose, then dove into the 29-degree water with his tether. Responders arrived from the D.C. and Arlington Fire Departments, including John Leck of Engine 3, who according to an official citation "without hesitation and regard for his own safety, secured a lifeline around his waist and entered the freezing water" to reach a drowning woman. Arland Williams, one of the injured passengers aboard Flight 90, stood on a sinking tail section of the plane and repeatedly handed the lifeline to other crash victims, sacrificing himself to save others, before finally disappearing beneath the water.

Park police risked their lives as they brought their helicopter low, scraping the wave tops with their landing skids. Seeing how one woman was unable to grab and hoist herself up the chopper's rescue line, Lenny Skutnik, office clerk, ripped off his coat and shoes, then dove into the Potomac in his shirt sleeves, swimming some thirty feet to reach a drowning Priscilla Tirado. "It was just too much to take," he said. "When she let go that last time … it was like a bolt of lightning or something hit me -- You've got to go get her."

Skutnik, who still works in the government printing office, doesn't consider himself an action figure. But two weeks after his daring save, he was invited to sit alongside Nancy Reagan for the President's State of the Union

Address. And subsequent Chief Execs, from Bill Clinton to Barak Obama, have followed suit each January, inviting common citizens who do uncommon deeds to stand and be recognized by Congress and the American people for their valor. Honorees have ranged from Daniel Hernandez, a young, gay, Hispanic aide who helped save Congresswoman Gabrielle Gifford's life after she was struck by an assassin's bullet, to Wesley Autrey, a New York City construction worker deemed the "Subway Superman" when he threw himself over an epileptic man who had fallen to the tracks, shielding both as the train hurtled above their prone bodies.

These exemplary Samaritans are all known, among the Washington press corps, as "Lenny Skutniks."

The question is, what creates a Lenny Skutnik or motivates an otherwise ordinary person to risk her life for others? Medical scientists have one possible explanation. Joseph LeDoux, a brain researcher at the Center for Natural Science at NYU, suggests that behavior of the kind seen at Flight 90 may arise from the amygdala, one of the primitive regions of grey matter that governs much of our emotional life. LeDoux discovered that information from our sense organs--the eyes, ears and nose--can travel neural pathways that bypass the cerebral cortex and go straight to the centers of arousal. Without stopping to think about it, we see what needs to be done and act. That would account for statements like Mr. Skutnik's, who following his swim in the Potomac remarked that "It's something I never thought I would do." Non-thinking, irrational impulses might explain the dashing, headlong quality of some heroic actions. But if that is the complete story, then heroism is largely a reflex, no more praiseworthy or inspiring than the dilation of a pupil under a beam of light, or the jerking knee which kicks the air when struck by a rubber mallet.

A more satisfying explanation, for me, comes from the philosopher Schopenhauer, who said that such acts of self-emptying spring from the metaphysical insight which seizes the mind in the moment of crisis that all life is one. In the extremity of facing our own demise or witnessing the peril of others, we see what life truly is: a single and indivisible unity, manifested in many forms, but equally precious in every one. The hero or heroine, then, is able to lay down her individual existence because she understands that life does not belong to her, rather she belongs to life. Through risking everything, the hero becomes the vehicle and messenger for a larger, more generous vision of who we are, why we are here, and what it means to be human.

I thought about this the night of September 11. That unforgettable morning, thousands of souls had been crushed and incinerated, including hundreds of firefighters who raced into the burning twin towers of lower Manhattan even as others rushed away. Gathered with other faith leaders and neighbors from the wider community that same evening, I wept. All day I had been holding tears inside, in shock, occupied with the details of planning a citywide vigil. But as I looked out across the faces of the crowd that filled my church that night, the gates opened. Our kinship was palpable. Each one there, friend or stranger, possessed a fragile life just like my own. While I didn't personally know any of the responders who perished that day, their deaths were no longer mere headlines, anonymous. The loss was immediate and personal. The attack was not just on New York City, or Washington, D.C., but on everyone, all of us, on our shared values and common humanity. As Schopenhauer understood, the horror brought us together.

"When a man becomes a fireman, his greatest act of heroism has been accomplished," declared the chief of New York City's Fire Department. "Whatever he does after that is all in the line of work." But can heroism ever part part of a job description, or is it rather a labor of love in the scriptural sense, "greater love hath no man than this ….?" Whatever sent New York's Bravest dashing up to the 78th floor was the same mighty flash that propelled Lenny into the water. And it was magnificent.

The Fireman Poems: Facing Our Addictions

The little town of Ossining, New York, sits on the shores of the Hudson River. It is home to Sing Sing prison, twenty-nine churches, one hundred fifty saloons, thirty-seven thousand residents and an unpaid fire department with nine companies numbering four-hundred seventy-five volunteers. Richard Smyth recalls that the fire service was an all male fraternity when his dad served a generation ago: part religion, part drinking hole, part man cave.

> *His father volunteered*
> *for Steamer Company No. 1*
> *The beer was cold,*
> *the heads were white*
> *and foamy,*
> *the mugs were*
> *icy.*
> *This is where his father came*
> *every week*
> *instead of going to church.*

There was actually a wet bar inside the station house where the only reliably sober guy was the one fixing drinks. The bartender drove the truck when the fire bell rang. One time, Richard remembers, his dad tumbled off the back of the engine on the way to a call. He was too inebriated to hang on.

This is where Richard spent his Sunday mornings, where instead of catechism, he was learning what ice meant and the definition of absolute zero, where he harbored a refrigerator inside his gut, where his eyes gazed out on the world like a snowman's: coals that were black and lifeless, coldly staring but not seeing. Numbed. As the adult child recalls,

> *Tomorrow sleeps on the couch*
> *like a drunken father ...*
> *Something is happening,*
> *he must wake up this father:*
> *life is happening:*
> *he grabs him by the shirt,*
> *shakes and shakes and shakes.*

There's no liquor at our Hondo station, but plenty of tippling off duty. I've sworn off the stuff during these three months at Fire School. I need the time to study and want to be clear-headed. But I'm no teetotaler. Like a lot of firefighters, I drink too much, too often. It started when my mother died. Loss accumulates. You want something to dull the ache. Or maybe that's just an excuse. The truth is,

[73]

you get hooked. Alcohol is seductive. You start to crave it when you're feeling good ("let's celebrate") and thirst still more when you're feeling bad. The older I get, the more frequently I visit the bottle.

I happened across Richard's verse by accident, then learned we actually have mutual friends as well as some theology in common. Both of us admire Teilhard de Chardin, the paleontologist priest who blended his science with a mystical vision of the divine as primordial energy. "In the beginning were neither cold nor darkness; there was Fire." Like his mentor, Smyth believes that heat is the imposition of order on chaos. Energized matter organizes itself into living forms, from the cellular level to planetary systems. Radiance is not just an attribute of God. Incandescence is the Creator.

> *Astronomers speak of black holes*
> *that suck the light from the universe,*
> *cosmic child drinking a sweet milk.*
> *They theorize also the white hole,*
> *the place where light emerges,*
> *the birth of light:*
> *god-hole,*
> *breast of energy,*
> *life filling the spaces.*

The Fireman, for Richard, has become the symbol for restoration and redemption: the individual who burns like a small sun, overcoming the forces of darkness and entropy. The Fireman is one who channels synergy, lights a candle, tends the spark.

A teacher of English in Haverhill, Massachusetts, Richard edits a literary magazine called *Albatross*. Another journal published his Snowman Poems, while the magazine *Color Wheel* printed his Fireman Poems in their entirety. Together the series describes his own personal trajectory from cold dwarf to nova. With the help of the twelve steps and support from his local Unitarian Universalist church--a congregation broad-minded enough to mix Jesus with astrophysics and Buckminster Fuller--Richard is in recovery from his alcoholism like who father, who finally achieved sobriety a decade before his death. In his poem "The Fireman is Burning Bridges," he writes:

> *There is a way to make sure*
> *you are always going forward.*
> *There is a way to make sure*
> *that nothing nothing nothing*
> *takes you back to that season of fatigue,*
> *that time of hibernation*
> *when the sun was too far away*
> *to make a difference:*
> *burn the bridges of addiction,*

watch in wonder as smoke fills the air.

Don't we all know the Snowman, the glacial self that sedates and negates? There are so many ways to freeze out experience. Booze. Blaming. Avoidance. Anesthetizing the soul. Yet there are also stratagems to stay warm and connected, to hold heat loss at bay. Poetry. Prayer. Intimacy. Commitment. Insulating ourselves from the pain and the passion only hastens the big chill. Fire exists by burning.

The Fireman has burned candles before.
He knows how quickly wax melts,
knows the physics of energy transfer.

Yet he still does it: he still burns
both ends, never wondering
where the energy will come from
to wake up tomorrow.

Perhaps it is possible to burn more slowly.
Perhaps it is possible
to go the distance.

Perhaps. Yet to me, the distance often feels more like a back-and-forth rather than any straight line procession, pulled in opposing directions between fire and ice, the binary stars that govern our human orbit.

It's getting late. Time is short. How do the constellations align tonight? I pour the coffee, forgo the wine.   As long as we can, we stoke the inward flame, forgive our fathers, turn our grief to verse, join a church or volunteer with a steamer brigade, clinging fast to the back of the engine, trying hard to stay on the wagon … always knowing the next crazy curve may be the final spin that pitches us into ashes and old night.

Karma: What Goes Around Comes Around

While I didn't know any firefighters before I joined Hondo, I am related to a few. In fact, my wife's grandfather was chief of the company in the little town of Nanticoke, Pennsylvania, a center of America's coal industry a century ago, where both her parents were born. The cast iron bell from the fire house, a good heavy alarm that summoned the citizenry in time of danger, remains in our family to this day.

Mining was dirty work. Great-grandfather Balliet died of black lung, as did my wife's great uncle Ellis. Grandmother Jeannette told stories of her younger brother Evan, who was so small when he trudged off to the pit that his lunch bucket literally dragged the ground and who perished in an accident at age fourteen. Lewis Jones had a wooden leg and a mangled arm from his mining mishaps, for which he received a compensation check of $500, enough to build a simple house without heating or plumbing, which is where my wife's father grew up.

Percy, his dad, was on duty during the so-called St. Patrick's Day flood of 1936, when the Susquehanna River crested at over thirty-three feet. Heavy snowpack washed down by two inches of unseasonably warm spring rain made the storm the Katrina of its day. Mayor Fiorello La Guardia of New York sent three fire engines and thirty-eight pumpers to assist with the disaster. Workers from the Civilian Conservation Corps joined the relief effort. Even the President, FDR, visited the stricken Wyoming Valley. But the heavy lifting fell to the local responders. There were over fifteen thousand recorded rescues and, amazingly, only nine documented deaths. One of them was the fire chief from Nanticoke, Percy L. Jones.

Memories differ, but it was a water-borne disease like cholera or typhus that killed him. The chief and his crew of volunteers had been at work in the cemetery, burying the coffins that floated up through the soggy soil to create a cesspool of contagion when the waters rose. He would have his own plot in that graveyard at the age of forty-five.

For the family, in the midst of the Great Depression, it was a calamity. My wife's dad, just eighteen and a freshman at Bucknell, dropped out of school to support his mother and younger siblings. His dreams of becoming a concert pianist were dashed. He worked in a bank. The offer from the Army Air Force to pay for flying lessons seemed a godsend to the young man. Within a short time, he was flying bombing runs over Tokyo, navigating a B-29 Super Fortress, helping to win the war and also inventing a deadly maelstrom never before witnessed: the man made fire storm.

The year was 1945, and just a month before Allied Forces had created a similar inferno in Dresden, Germany. Hundreds of tons of bunker-busting bombs and incendiaries sucked every wisp of oxygen from the air, suffocating victims before toasting them to cinders, as thermal columns rose miles into the sky. Protected in a subterranean hog barn that had been converted to a barracks ("slaughterhouse five"), a young P.O.W. named Kurt Vonnegut survived the fury that killed an estimated 25,000 others. Unlike Nanticoke, the corpses in this case were too numerous for burial. Vonnegut and other prisoners were set to burning bodies with flame throwers.

The future author never forgot. He idolized the figure who represented the antithesis of raining brimstone from the sky: the fireman. In his novel *God Bless You, Mr. Rosewater*, he celebrated Eliot, an eccentric billionaire who devotes his vast fortune to aiding the undeserving ne'er-do-wells of the little Indiana town where he sets up shop. The tiny office of the Rosewater Foundation is decorated with little more than Eliot's certificate as a notary public and the yellow slicker and red helmet of the fire volunteer. "Eliot was a Fire Lieutenant. He could easily have been a Captain or Chief, since he was a devoted and skilful Fireman, and had given the Fire Department six new engines besides."

For Eliot, firefighting was an act of soulwork or atonement. During the war, leading a platoon of American G.I.s into a Bavarian clarinet factory supposedly infested with S.S. troops, the decorated vet bayonets three Germans wearing gas masks who turn out not to be soldiers at all. Instead, he has mistakenly gutted three firemen. The trauma leaves Eliot with a monomaniacal desire to help people instead of hurting them--parceling out kindness to one and all, not because they are deserving, but simply because they are human. It leaves many wondering whether Eliot is a saint or bodhisattva or just unhinged.

The author's alter-ego--science fiction writer Kilgore Trout--comments on the fundamental soundness of the philanthropist's kindness-toward-all approach:

Your devotion to volunteer fire departments is very sane, Eliot, for they are, when the alarm goes off, almost the only examples of enthusiastic unselfishness to be seen in this land. They rush to the rescue of any human being, and count not the cost. The most contemptible man in town, should his contemptible house catch fire, will see his enemies put the fire out. And, as he pokes through the ashes for the remains of his contemptible possessions, he will be comforted and pitied by no less than the Fire Chief.

Trout spreads his hands in a gesture of respect, indicating all the members of the fire service. "There we have people treasuring people as people"

Like the hero of his novel, Kurt Vonnegut himself served as a fire and rescue volunteer, Badge No. 55, in the village of Alplaus, near the General Electric Plant in Schenectady where he worked after the war. Weeks before his death, the celebrated author sent his old compatriots in the Capitol Region Fire District a framed, silkscreen print emblazoned with the symbol of the firefighter's Maltese Cross and a quotation: "I cannot imagine a more stirring symbol of man's humanity to man than a fire engine." On the back, he penned a note.

Dear Alplaus Firemen: I was once one of you, way back in the early 1950s and I give you this as a token of my respect for all you are and do.

In some ironic manner, my father-in-law contributed to all that, I believe. Percy L. Jones and Kurt Vonnegut, Jr. were part of the same karass - in the fictional religion of "Bokononism" a network of unrelated individuals whose destinies are nonetheless inexplicably linked. The fire chief's sacrifice led the son to become an expert at dropping high explosives, whose havoc in turn created another fireman. Each played their karmic role,

[82]

while some cosmic circuit got completed. The moral compass turned full circle.

When I buried my wife's dad the aviator at Arlington National Cemetery, a military honor guard fired a rifle salute. When Kurt Vonnegut died the following year, the bells at the Alplaus Fire House tolled the traditional cadence to mark a passing comrade. Which was the finer tribute?

The soldier and the fireman. I have to honor them both.

America's Fiery Fourth: Where In Blazes Are The Patriots?

The Fourth of July means fireworks to most Americans. It should be a day to celebrate firefighters, too, and commemorate values that reflect what's best in our national character.

Most people know, for instance, that Benjamin Franklin, who helped draft the Declaration of Independence, was also a Founding Father of the fire service. As publisher of the Pennsylvania Gazette, he dedicated numerous articles to preventing and putting out blazes like one that burned much of Philadelphia's wharf in 1730. At the time, some cities like Boston boasted "Fire Clubs" that responded with pumps and buckets to the private emergencies of their members or paid subscribers. But Franklin envisioned a community service that would battle conflagrations whenever and wherever they occurred. At his urging, the Union Fire Company was formed in 1735, staffed entirely by volunteers, the first public fire department in the American colonies.

He had the highest praise for those daring responders who risked life and limb on behalf of their neighbors.

[84]

See there a gallant Man who has rescu'd Children from the Flames! — Another receives in his Arms a poor scorch'd Creature escaping out at a Window! — Another is loaded with Papers and the best Furniture, and secures them for the Owner. — What daring Souls are cutting away the flaming Roof to stop the Fires Progress to others! — How vigorously do these brave Fellows hand along the Water and work the Engines, and assist the Ladders; and with what Presence of Mind, Readiness and Clearness, do these fine Men observe, advise and direct. Here are Heroes and effective Men fit to compose the Prime of an Army, and to either lay or defend a Siege or Storm.

Firefighters for him embodied selflessness and practical altruism: virtues he supposed would attract the finer sort. There were twenty signatories on the original roster for Franklin's Union Fire Company, including silversmith Philip Syng, who crafted the inkstand that would be used when signing the Declaration of Independence and the U.S. Constitution. Charles Willing, another of the organizing band, was mayor of Philadelphia and would send his son Thomas as a delegate to the Continental Congress.

Soon other companies were established on the same model, often with prominent citizens in the lead. George Washington, Thomas Jefferson, Samuel Adams, John Hancock, Alexander Hamilton and Paul Revere were all active in their local fire companies. The wealthy Hancock purchased and donated a fire engine to his native city, while two of Revere's apprentices, skilled craftsmen, designed and built pumpers themselves. Not to be outdone, George Washington for eighteen pounds and ten shillings procured an engine for the Friendship Fire Company where he was a member in Alexandria, Virginia, in 1775, the year before he took up command of the American regiments.

Early fire companies were laboratories of democracy, where men elected their own leaders and gained both organizational and tactical skills. As Franklin observed, "the Men belonging to the Engine, at their Quarterly Meetings, discourse of Fires, of the Faults committed at some, the good Management in some Cases at others, and thus communicating their Thoughts and Experience they grow wise in the Thing, and know how to command and to execute in the best manner upon every Emergency." Fighting fires was perfect training for the bigger fight to come.

During the American Revolution, firefighters were generally exempt from military service due to their essential function, yet many served with distinction, like soldiers of Philadelphia's Hibernia Fire Company, whom Washington thanked after the war for their "spirit and bravery, which will ever do honor to them." Some who didn't carry guns, such as Quaker George Emlen (one of the original members of Philadelphia's Union Fire Company and a pacifist on principle) provided firewood for the troops near Valley Forge.

Within fifty years of independence, women would join the fire forces also. The first recorded female volunteer was Molly Williams, an African American slave who joined New York's Oceanus Fire Company in 1818. Two years later, Marina Betts signed up with her local brigade in Pittsburgh, where she became famous for dumping buckets of water on male bystanders who refused to join in the work of extinguishing the flames!

By the middle of the nineteenth century, Walt Whitman, the most democratic of poets, would eulogize the bravery of these volunteers in his tribute to "Heroes."

I am the mashed fireman with breast-bone broken,
Tumbling walls buried me in their debris,
Heat and smoke I inspired, I heard the yelling
shouts of my comrades,
I heard the distant click of their picks and shovels.

As much as their physical courage and sacrifice, the poet admired their robust swag and swagger: "The march of firemen in their own costumes, the play of masculine muscle through clean-setting trowsers and waist-straps."

Before cowboys or astronauts, America fell in love with the fire corps.

What finer expression of patriotism than the fire department? As a volunteer, I vow to serve my countrymen and women regardless of race or religion, whether they are rich or poor, gay or straight, whenever the need arises. Here in Santa Fe County, our patrons include Anglos, Hispanics and four Native pueblos in a town where million dollar homes sit aside barrios filled with rusting trailers. Everyone is treated as an equal. Americans don't trust politicians or Congress much these days. Faith in government is in decline. Prisons have been turned over to money-making corporations. Public schools compete against charters and exclusive academies. Independent contractors are replacing the military. Right-wingers want to turn Social Security into a personal savings account. But nobody suggests privatizing the fire department. It is one of the few institutions that reminds our fragmented nation that we are still one people, all in this together.

In the *Federalist Papers*, Founder and firefighter John Jay wrote, "Among the many objects to which a wise and free people find it necessary to direct their attention, that of providing for their safety seems to be the first." Today John Jay College offers degrees in fire science to those who want to follow his advice. To learn more about becoming part of this honorable and fiery tradition, visit the fire station nearest you. Applicants are welcomed. Good hearted, hard-working men and women are needed.

What better way to demonstrate your love of country or celebrate the Fourth?

Living Long, Living Well: Cultivating Reasonably Bad Habits

Who wants to live to be a hundred? The question crossed my mind as I was helping the medics with Sebastian, who had tripped outside his home and who told us he had been born the year the Great War started. Woodrow Wilson was President then. Henry Ford had just introduced the model T. The Panama Canal opened for business that year, too. Sebastian was obviously a survivor. No one knew how long he had been lying there, in the cool of the night. A neighbor phoned. We helped him to his feet and sat him down on a rock. I told him to take it slow. We were in no hurry. Amazingly, he was not hypothermic but alert and reluctant to go to the hospital, yet gentlemanly about it, polite and uncomplaining. We sent him to the emergency room anyway.

I liked his manner and, without really knowing him, sensed that he had aged well, like a finely-tailored suit or some classic car (Packard or Bentley), full of character, keeping up appearances, self-possessed despite the embarrassment of not remembering how he'd tumbled or the rush of responders round about. From his professorial glasses and turns of speech, I guessed Sebastian had a bookish or contemplative turn of mind. He set me to philosophizing.

Sebastian reminds me that "firefighter" is not a permanent identity. Sometimes in this life we get to be the rescuer and then we become the rescued. A few years from now, should I last so long, I will be just like Sebastian, though probably grouchier. Because aging adroitly is a gift. Allowing ourselves to receive help, to be dependent on others, admitting our frailties, leaning on the strong shoulder, is not easy for any of us, and maybe especially hard for males. Guys are trained to be the tower of strength, which can be dangerous, actuarially speaking.

Most firefighters retire before they reach fifty, for good reason. On average, they die early, and are four times more likely than others to contract various cancers, with an on-the-job death rate three times that of less dangerous occupations. Testicular tumors are especially common. (When exiting a burning building, don't grab your whizzer to take a leak, I was warned. The buckles and fly on your bunker trousers have been covered with contaminants. Wash your hands before, as well as after, going to the bathroom).

These grim statistics may change. A generation ago, firefighters were far more casual about breathing smoke and airborne hazards. Wearing a helmet blackened with soot was like wearing a black belt: the emblem of a ninja. Grime was macho. In that era, it was easier to get away with such posturing, too. Homes were mostly built of wood, metal, and other natural products, whereas today's dwellings are filled with adhesives, plastics and foams that burn dirty. Construction is more poisonous.

Still, apparently real men inhale, 'cause lots of firefighters are smokers, as well. Many of the guys I know (including me) ride motorcycles. Bad Habits 'R Us. The snack drawer at our station is stuffed with Oreos and donuts are on the menu every Saturday morning when we arrive to inspect the engines. Bacon (a known carcinogen) is a staple.

Firefighters are habituated to adrenaline. Taking chances draws us like a chimney draws smoke. Despite that, some manage to reach century mark. Most centenarians are retirees, but Vincent Dransfield is one of the exceptions, one hundred years old and still chasing blazes, making him the nation's oldest active firefighter.

"This guy in Arkansas had me beat by three years, but he died two years ago," Dransfield bragged at a birthday celebration where he commemorated seventy-five years of continuous duty with his New Jersey township. When he joined the department in 1939, the company in his home of Little Falls still used horses to pull the engines.

On scene, Dransfield isn't climbing ladders or manning the nozzle anymore, but can still operate the pumps.

Asked for the secret to his endurance, Dransfield attributed his longevity to Ovaltine, one glass every morning for the last sixty years. I don't have a death wish, but do like my morning coffee. Barley malt extract, milk serum concentrate and fat-reduced cocoa powder may be a fountain of youth. But I'll stick with stronger libations.

Existence is a perilous affair, which implies a tension between living long and living well. Finding the proper balance between the two requires learning to manage risk. In Fire School, we were taught to risk a lot to save a lot--for instance, venturing into a burning basement when there may be live victims trapped inside--but to gamble little or nothing when the stakes are comparatively low. This is a good rule for attacking a smoldering warehouse--no one should risk their neck to salvage some worthless property--but not such a useful maxim for living. Because life means more than mere survival. It entails more than minimizing hazards. It involves willingness to fail, experimentation, creative destruction, leaps of faith that sometimes fall flat.

Falling on your face literally, like Sebastian.

The truth is that firefighters spend more time battling gravity than fighting heat and smoke. Medical emergencies constitute most of our calls, and the majority of those are man down. Usually there is an elder who can't get up off the floor.

It reminds me that aging typically has two stages: *old* and *old, old,* differentiated partly by our tolerance for tripping. For many, old age is one of the happiest times of life. Like my friends at Hondo, you can race Harleys, travel to Patagonia or Peru, start up a new enterprise peddling solar cells, even drive fire trucks. Do the bucket list. Spend your children's inheritance. When you stumble, you can pick yourself up again. Then comes decrepitude or old old, which is about renunciation and abstention. Reduced salt, reduced mobility, reduced risk, reduced expectations. Not taking any spills. Ovaltine instead of Old Granddad. That's the real challenge, which requires a different kind of strength: not putting out the blaze, but living with aplomb and wisdom even when the embers are burning low.

If that day ever comes, I hope I can manage as graciously as Sebastian, an old, old man but still a model and mentor to those younger: poised, proper, and teaching the rescuers how to be rescued with elan. One hundred birthdays in the rearview, but still a class act.

Hot Stuff: Service Is More Sweat Than Glory

Last night my classmates and I celebrated our formal graduation from Volunteer Fire Academy. Thirteen out of the original eighteen who enrolled matriculated. Unlike lesser souls who dropped by the wayside, I qualified as Firefighter 1, certified by the National Fire Protection Association to enter burning buildings and slay the dragon--a goal that a few months ago I never dreamed of putting on my life list.

I felt both done and done in.

I was exhausted even before the ceremony began, having sweated three hot hours on the highway tarmac hauling hose. A Ford Explorer with Arizona plates had flipped when the trailer it was towing went out of control. The brown Jayco Camper and its contents were scattered along the shoulder as if hit by a monster cyclone. Mattresses, sleeping bags, propane bottles, baby wipes, rag dolls, stuffed animals and Disney DVDs littered the sagebrush, along with shreds of insulation, splintered two-by-twos, and other scraps of the caravan. Somehow the three occupants of the car, a two-year-old girl and her grandparents, survived the mayhem. I was backing up my fellow firefighter Catherine on the nozzle, drenching the whole scene in Class A foam as gas dribbled to the ground, preventing any ignition while EMT's pulled the living from the wreckage, then waiting for the Department of Transportation to arrive with a dump truck and front-end loader. Not enough debris remained to tow. It had to be scooped up wholesale.

This felt like the real thing: what I'd trained for. The exams, the burn building, the skills testing never amounted to much. Socorro, where we practiced with live fire, was a little like some of the student apartments I remembered living in: dark, smelly, and dirty. Unlike those student rentals, the burn building at least had heat.

Was it frightening or exhilarating, walking into a blazing building? No, mostly just draining, physically punishing. I was swaddled like a mummy in a thick thermal casing designed to keep fire out yet by the same token sealing in the products of my own internal combustion. Nose running. Glands perfusing. Even with SCBA (Self-Contained Breathing Apparatus), sucking compressed air, I was coughing fumes afterward for two days. Don't eat more than your mask can hold, the Captain warned the cadets before lunchtime. All excretions must stay within that hermetically sealed cocoon.

Hondo's suits are black, just like those of the NYC Fire Department, because back in 1974, when our district was founded, that's where our equipment came from, hand-me-downs from the Big Apple. Here in the Southwest, the gear soaks up the sun.

And there were rays aplenty. Nothing I did on the interstate yesterday was especially taxing. I didn't run up 110 flights of stairs - which is how firefighters commemorate their brethren who died in the World Trade Towers. But I was spent. I could hardly stay awake through the speeches at commencement. I do recall that we pledged to uphold the Constitution and the laws of New Mexico. But only one other bit stuck with me, a quote from actor Bradley Whitford (a.k.a. Josh Lyman of the "West Wing" series) that was part of our invocation:

Infuse your life with action. Don't wait for it to happen. Make it happen. Make your own future. Make your own hope. Make your own love. And whatever your beliefs, honor your creator, not by passively waiting for grace to come down from upon high, but by doing what you can to make grace happen... yourself, right now, right down here on Earth.

Is that what I'm doing, making grace happen? Infusing life with action? It felt a little like that yesterday on the highway, being part of a team trained and equipped to save lives amid the biggest FUBAR imaginable. A little friction, a spark, would have turned that Explorer into a

[98]

crematory, with occupants still inside. These are the situations you prepare for. These are the moments when firefighters earn their acclaim. Yet I didn't feel like such hot stuff.

Mostly I just felt hot.

Drinking from the Fire Hose: Going Slow To Go Fast and Other Parables

I have already forgotten most of what I learned in Fire Academy. The curriculum was like a drink from a high pressure nozzle: a deluge of information. But there are some lessons that stay with you--easy to remember even if they take a lifetime to learn.

Go slow to go fast. During World War II, Navy fighter pilots supposedly had a wristwatch attached to the yoke that controlled the plane's pitch and roll. Their first protocol when initiating emergency procedures was to stop everything and wind the watch. It sounds nuts. But by taking that extra moment, the flyboys gave themselves time to pause and think: just long enough so that could act rather than merely react to the crisis at hand.

The same rule applies on the fireground. When driving to a scene, even with sirens screaming, it is smart to slow down. The few seconds you save by speeding or racing through intersections against the light are nothing compared to the risk of a collision. And don't rush putting on your gear. There was a young guy, Frank, at the Academy who could don his boots, coat, helmet, gloves, mask, hood and compressed-air harness in about the same

[100]

time I required to kick off my street shoes and start getting dressed. But trying to be as quick as Frank just got me tangled, mentally as well as physically. Taking the task methodically, one-step-at-a-time, proved to be the most efficient way to get things done.

Slow and steady wins the race. Jocelyn Davis and Tom Atkinson make the same point in the Harvard Business Review. "In our study of 343 businesses, the companies that embraced initiatives and chose to go, go, go to try to gain an edge ended up with lower sales and operating profits than those that paused at key moments to make sure they were on the right track."

Profit from this advice. Whether you are running a business, flying a plane, chartering a vacation (how many cities can you see in six days?) or wooing a woman, fastest is not always best.

Think Before You Speak. Communications at an emergency scene mostly occur over the radio. Dispatchers may get notice of three or four crises within minutes, sending criss-crossing alarms all over the county. In addition, districts like Hondo have their own tactical channels to coordinate the half dozen or so volunteers arriving to any given incident. It gets confusing. If we all talk at once, or fail to follow some simple guidelines of courtesy and brevity, the babel becomes intolerable as multiple individuals chatter and one message cuts into another.

That happened on a call where I happened to be driving the ambulance to an accident scene with multiple victims. Paul, our EMT-Basic on board, kept getting "stepped on" each time he radioed to ask whether other medical units were on the way. He had to make a quick decision, whether to transport a critically injured child or hope that other advanced life support teams were close by. Bolloxed communication in this case, unfortunately, may have cost a human life.

For clarity's sake, police, firefighters and other emergency responders now avoid "ten codes" and other specialized jargon. Plain English is preferred. But the most important rule I learned was to think before I speak. On the radio in my car, there is a button I have to push to transmit. Before depressing it, I formulate in my mind precisely what I need to say.

There is a delay of about two seconds between the moment you depress the key and the instant you can send your voice sailing over the airwaves. I don't think the manufacturer designed it that way, but how often I wish I had a built-in regulator which required me to pause before opening my mouth.

Have you ever blurted out statements you wished you could retract? Next time you are in a business meeting, or gossiping at church, or about to snarl into the phone with the clerk who lost your order, imagine that you are miked and about to go on-air, county wide. Choose your words with care. As the King James puts it, "Even a fool, when he holdeth his peace, is counted wise."

Pay attention. Stay frosty. Be alert. Buddhists call this mindfulness. Firefighters call the condition of constant vigilance "situational awareness." By either name, it suggests cultivating a consciousness that is cool, observant, curious and always noticing who (or what) is around you, as if your life depended on it.

Matsura, Zen tradition tells us, wanted to become a great swordsman, so he apprenticed himself to Banzo, the best dueller in the country. For three years, the student swept floors, washed dishes and performed other menial duties until the master was convinced of his sincerity. Then, one day while Matsura was gardening, Banzo leapt out from behind a tree and gave his apprentice a sharp whack with a heavy wooden sword. The next day, the surprise attack came in the kitchen. After that, the blows continued to fall whenever least expected. Matsura learned to live on the balls of his feet, in eternal readiness: a body with no thought or desire of its own, but prepared to respond to whatever peril the moment might bring. Banzo finally saw that his pupil was fit to begin lessons, and Matsura soon became the greatest samurai in Japan.

"Look up, look down, look all around," was the drill we learned in Fire School. Situational awareness on a wildfire means continuously monitoring weather, terrain, fuel loads, escape routes, and the totality of your environment, without allowing the blister forming inside your boot to completely claim your focus. No tunnel vision or daydreaming allowed. Be fully present to whatever is happening, moment-to-moment.

Mindfulness can literally save your life in a swordfight or on the fireground. But even when the dangers facing you are less immediately threatening (boredom, self-absorption, distraction, escapism, aimless drifting and the other psychological pitfalls of daily living) the warrior spirit may give you a life worth saving.

Fighting fires is one of the hardest jobs I have ever tackled. There is so much to absorb: building construction and flashovers; electrical fires and gas leaks; weather forecasting and map reading; oxidizers and asphyxiants; how to tie a bowline and operate a smoke ejector; even what to do when someone's eyeball pops out! (Put it in a paper cup and wait for the real docs to arrive, according to our textbook, although my sister-in-law the physician says just apply a little spit and reinsert the orb into the socket).

Yet the last lesson I'm learning, humility, is the hardest of all. The base of knowledge and skills is simply too big for this Harvard grad to master. I try to be minimally competent and some days that's a stretch. But I have confidence in the chain of command. I know I am part of a team. Woody is a genius with radios. John can fix anything mechanical. Hersch and David are tops on emergency medicine. Mike knows how to take command. I know just enough to trust that they know what they know, and I show up (which should never be underrated). I do not have to master everything or do it all. Because no task performed alone will finally make a difference.

Firefighter Nation: Beyond Looking Out For Number One

Where would we be without volunteers? During my career as a clergyman, I learned how many helping hands it takes to run a church. Sunday School teachers, choir members, Habitat hammerers, and more. Nearly everyone in my congregation volunteered around town, too. They organized art festivals, toiled on the zoning commission, coached youth league soccer, and were friends of the library. "Leadership" has been defined as what you have left over to give back to the world, after your own personal needs have been attended to. By that definition, most of us are capable of being leaders, and America is led by volunteers.

Before I joined Hondo, I never realized the fire service is mostly unpaid, which is amazing considering that it provides such essential functions: EMS, search and rescue, fire suppression, motor vehicle extrication, controlling burns in wildland and forest. Before moving to the rural edges of New Mexico, I'd always lived in cities where firefighters are remunerated. But unlike cops or our country's "volunteer army" (whose base pay is rapidly outpacing civilian salaries), most firefighters actually work for very little or nothing. Frequently they have to fundraise to purchase their own equipment. I'm mostly volunteer but not totally: since graduating from the Academy, the county gives me eleven dollars for gas and expenses each time I go out on call.

Some calls take hours, like the garage fire that was my first real burn. Two cars were torching inside, with flames shooting up from a collapsed roof and unidentified stuff (tires? aerosols?) exploding in the heat. We couldn't get the big engines up the narrow mountain driveway and were limited for water, trying to contain the cinders that were singeing the forested hillside above. When we finally did lay a water line, the steep slope quickly turned into a quagmire. I slipped in the mud, hauling hose up the incline, staggering under the weight of my gear. Then re-loading the trucks and cleaning our masks back at the station, getting ready for next time, took nearly as long as extinguishing the blaze. I might have been making two bucks an hour.

I wasn't doing it for cash. Yet I've never felt prouder of any eleven dollars I ever earned. Firefighters put themselves out there for a variety of motives: for the excitement, the camaraderie, or like me for the satisfaction of feeling that this old body can still function after more than six decades of use and abuse. But whatever their reasons for signing up, they comprise a small nation.

According to the U.S. Fire Administration, there are approximately 1,140,750 active firefighters in the United States. More than two-thirds of those are unpaid, which is a big number.

For comparison, five states have smaller populations. As a group, volunteer firefighters outnumber the residents of major cities like Boston, Atlanta, Seattle or Denver. Even without the incentive of a paycheck, they are bigger than the U.S. Army. Linked in an old-fashioned bucket brigade, a human chain of fire service volunteers would stretch across five hundred miles … from Boston to Bethesda, or from Taos to Tucson.

There are just over thirty thousand fire departments in the United States. Of those, 19,807 are all volunteer, with almost a third of those staffed like our station at Hondo, where the county maintains two paid paramedics, supplemented by about thirty men and women who are non-career, but not unprofessional.

Both career and unpaid staff are held to same standards, take the same risks, perform the same tasks, and work side by side. We are a unit, and I appreciate the pros who finally appeared to help mop up the garage. But when volunteers are the first to arrive at a fire or accident scene, a guy not much different than me (or at some point it could even be me) will take command and may be directing career firemen (even those of higher rank) who show up to assist. I can't think of any other line of work, skilled or unskilled, where this is the case.

Volunteers sustain most of the casualties in the line of duty, just because there are more of them. Imagine if America had a million volunteer nurses, or math teachers, or conservation workers, or a million home health aides or pediatricians other helping professionals who were willing not only to donate time but actually put their lives on the line for others.

Instead of asking kids, "What do you want to be when you grow up?" we should be asking young people the question, "How do you want to serve when you're ready?" I remember Colman McCarthy, the peace activist and Washington Post columnist, sharing that observation when he spoke at our church some years back. Our society puts so much emphasis on earning a living and preparing students to enter the labor force. From an early age, we learn the importance of self-promotion and marketing. Success is defined by job title and paycheck.

But there is another definition, because deep down people want to feel their lives matter and their work makes a difference. Because along with the selfish, prudential part of every person, there's also a selfless component to each of us: some deep down yearning to spend ourselves for the common good, to risk for others, to go beyond looking out for number one, even to dare to be a little sacrificial now and then. People aren't all mean, or cynical, or disillusioned, or not only that, not all the time. They are also idealistic and generous, loving and public-spirited. And that courageous, caring, self-transcending dimension of our humanity is very powerful, strong enough even to send men and women racing into the flames if need be.

What's the evidence? Eight hundred thousand fire house volunteers.

Dream A Little Dream: Answers To The Great Examination

When I was a pastor, I had a recurrent dream. It was Sunday morning and I had forgotten my sermon or couldn't find the door to the sanctuary. I haven't had that dream in years. But recently, I dreamt that I was on the fireground and couldn't find the right connector for the supply hose.

This feels like progress. Some part of my psyche is giving a whole new answer to the question that launched me on my late life adventure with Hondo. Who am I? The answer comes: A fireman.

Anxiety dreams are common. A frequent one, for me, involves being in a classroom, preparing to take a test. My wife has had the same dream, as well as a lot of other people I know.

If you're like me, your heart is racing and your mind is confused, because you haven't attended lectures all semester. You haven't done the reading. You're not entirely sure of the subject matter you are being quizzed on. What was being taught? Who was giving the lessons? What were you supposed to learn? No answers are provided, With a sense of approaching catastrophe, I realize that although I am about to be tested, I have no clue how to pass.

What is the meaning of this peculiar dream? I was always a pretty good student and never that nervous about exams in real life. Why does it seem to be a fixture in our collective unconscious? Surely it involves something more than lingering classroom jitters.

I think the dream is about the Great Examination each of us must face. The items on the exam are the Ultimate Questions: Who am I? What do I want? What am I afraid of? Where is my own highest good calling me?

This is not just a dream about academic anxieties or forgetting the date of the Magna Carta. It is about forgetting our own reason for being.

We each have one lifetime (that we know about) and no make-ups are allowed. Is it any wonder we are all tossing and turning in our sleep? When the alarm sounds and the bell tolls, we have to be ready to give some account of ourselves. We have to answer for how we chose to spend our time.

How will you respond? Does your path have a heart? Did you help somebody?

When asked, I won't be sorry to say that I spent my golden years fighting fires.

Other Books by Gary Kowalski

The Souls of Animals (New World Library)

Goodbye Friend: Healing Wisdom For Anyone Who Has Ever Lost A Pet (New World Library)

The Bible According To Noah: Theology As If Animals Mattered (Lantern Books)

Science and the Search for God (Lantern Books)

Blessings of the Animals: Celebrating Our Kinship With All Creation (Lantern Books)

Earth Day: An Alphabet Book (Skinner House)

Revolutionary Spirits: The Enlightened Faith of America's Founding Fathers (Bluebridge Publishing)

To contact the author, visit his website at
www.kowalskibooks.com

Made in the USA
Coppell, TX
18 July 2021

59156584R00069